"Pia's poems capture echoes from the past, reflections on the present and hope for the future. T.S. Eliot in "Four Quartets" writes:

> *"Footfalls echo in the memory*
> *Down the passage that we did not take*
> *Towards the door we never opened*
> *Into the rose-garden"*

The echoes from Pia's life as she reflects on the harsh realities of life's experiences and the disappointment of unfulfilled dreams can evoke our own echoes. But her poetry does more than dwell on life's disappointments; it also reveals the healing power of beauty glimpsed in nature and in life-affirming relationships. She moves from darkness to light; from despair to discovery and to the assured hope of the eternal "Rose Garden".

Robyn Claydon
Author/International speaker/Lecturer in Poetry/
Listed in the World's Who's Who of Women
and the Dictionary of Distinguished Leadership

"Great poems and perfect synesthesia (words and art)."

Koraljka
Artist and Illustrator

MY BEST POEMS

Part 2

The Challenge of

RELATIONSHIPS

© 2017 by Pia Horan-Gross

All rights reserved. No portion of this book may be reproduced, stored in a retrieval system, or transmitted in any form or by any means – electronic, mechanical, photocopy, recording, scanning, or other – except for brief quotations in critical reviews or articles, without the prior written permission of the author/self-publisher.

Unless otherwise noted, Scripture quotations are taken from the Holy Bible, New King James Version (NKJV) ® Copyright © 1982 by Thomas Nelson. Used by permission. All rights reserved.

ISBN 978-0-6480135-2-5

Table of Contents

FOREWORD	ix
A PRISTINE DAY	1
A SERIES OF BRIEF ENCOUNTERS	3
AN UNSURRENDERED HEART	6
AND I THOUGHT WE WERE FRIENDS!	7
AWAKENING	9
CARS PASSING	10
CAT AND MOUSE GAME	11
COCKROACHES	13
EMPTY	15
FAILED HARVEST	16
FEELING RAW	18
FOOL'S GOLD?	19
FRAGMENTS	20
FRIENDS	22
FUTURE RESPONSE	23
I KNOW	24
IMPROMPTU PERFORMANCE	26
JUST A DREAM	28
JUST FOR YOU	29
LIVING WITH UNEASINESS	31
LONGING	32

LOST DREAMS	34
MAKING A STAND	35
NO ONE TOLD ME BACK THEN	37
ODE TO A SOUL-MATE DREAM	38
PAIN	42
PLAYING WITH FIRE	43
PREDATOR	44
QUITTING	45
RED CARNATIONS	46
SECRET GARDEN	47
SIMPLY THANK YOU	49
SUBSTITUTES	51
TENTS DANCING	52
THE ALLY	54
THE APPENDIX	56
THE BIRTH	58
THE DIARY	60
THE GUARDIAN	63
THE IDOL	66
THE MASQUERADE	67
THE ROAD TO FREEDOM	69
THE TOXIC PARENT	71
TIME	73
TO WRITE POETRY	75

TOUCHED BY THE DIVINE	76
TRANSITION	79
TRUE VINE COMMUNITY	80
WAITING	83
WITHOUT A VOICE	84
YOU AND I	87

FOREWORD

*"Success is not final,
failure is not fatal:
it is the courage to continue
that counts."*

Winston Churchill

Some of us came into this world and continue living with a definite deficit in the area of love. We were either considered an inconvenience from the outset, too high a price to pay for someone's precious independence or else parented by parents who also had suffered from the same syndrome and therefore handicapped in the capacity to nurture and care for a little human, with huge, scary needs.

Such were my early beginnings and by the time I became a teenager, I battled with many "demons". Depression was one of them. My saving grace was the resolute determination that I wasn't going to spend the rest of my life staying emotionally handicapped.

Life inexorably moved forward and demanded decisions from me; decisions I had no real understanding about, except what the movie screen presented at that time, and to some extent still does. The stark reality though, presented on our screens these days regarding relationships, must seem even more confusing for those at the start of their adult lives!

One of the quotes from my poem "The Diary" sums up my life experience up to then: "experiences of pseudo-love and destructive love games. The fake is recognized only by knowing the real first."

Only since I have come to experience and learn about God's love for me in Christ and seen the reality of my consequent changed life, in every area, do I finally know what real love looks like. It is of course the purest love there is which, as Christians we are encouraged to follow and to show to the world. It requires putting self-centered needs second. It is amazing how life-giving, to others and to self, such practice, energized by His Spirit, really is!

I have not tried to hide how broken and self-absorbed I have been at times and still can be. It is part of my desire to reveal myself to my readers, warts and all! "We have this treasure in earthen vessels" we read in the Scriptures (2 Cor. 4:7). It is in our brokenness that we can identify with one another, yet we are called to become "like Him" (1 John 3:2) and that "He who has started a good work in you will complete it..." (Phil. 1:6).

My emotional life used to be like a roller coaster. Through an unceasing search after wholeness, by God's grace and much help and prayer from His people and those He put into my path, I have found ongoing peace and real, lasting joy!

I therefore thank first my God and Saviour for the gift of salvation, which is a privilege that has many layers to it, and every precious person whom God has used to bring greater insight and healing to me. I am forever indebted to you all! THANK YOU.

P.H.-G.

A PRISTINE DAY

Standing inside the beautiful inlet,
surrounded by shallow water,
not a soul around but us two,
you with your fishing rod.
The day is pristine,
a soft wind in the trees
A picture of perfection
except inside of us!

We've had another quarrel-
the second in a row.
Tempers frayed anew.
You, getting very bossy.
I, perplexed, incredulous,
then very, very blue.
It always seems to happen
when we're away together, on holidays!

My anger dissipated,
my stubborn will all but crushed.
I turn my back to you and battle tears,
conscious of this silent pathos,
reinforced by a sense of déjà vu.
What had promised to be paradise,
has turned into a prison of pain and fear.
And still more layers surfacing!

A legacy of distrust and pain
and a sense of impotence and rage
which, back then, I medicated with a vow:
"No one would ever boss me again!"
Then I go and marry you!
At times, kind and caring but also very controlling!
Suddenly, you're putting your arm around me…
Finally we listen and talk!

Cuttagee Lake, New South Wales,
April 2004

A SERIES OF BRIEF ENCOUNTERS

Out of the blue,
you came for a single visit.
You slept in the other bed,
in the guestroom of your father-in-law's pub.
That room was my nursery;
for lack of guests staying over.
My trunk in the corner,
inside all my toys and things,
quickly put out of sight, if need be-
a multi-functional set-up.
A little child in a large bed, in a big room.
We played a simple game of pop the cheeks,
resulting in peals of giggles and laughter.
I thought you finally loved me…

At seventeen, I had a dream.
With some help,
I managed to track you down.
A meeting ensued;
I tried so hard
to be pleasant, funny, pretty,
like going for an interview.
Your interest lasted a whole week.
Then, the all too familiar silence.
No answer to my letters.
No response to my wedding invitation.
I let go.
I stopped trying.
Stopped crying.

In my thirties,
with two young children,
newly divorced,
I happened to be in your area
(in your part of the globe).
I was told that you were very ill.
A meeting was arranged by someone.
I could find no pity when we met,
nor could I show a smile.
Just silent coldness.
The little child, now woman
had closed her door,
her once hopeful heart
had turned to ice.

The last meeting between us
was in a dream.
You approached me.
Your pleading eyes
asked for forgiveness
for the indifference
the neglect,
the failure of a father
to acknowledge his daughter.
I just turned away –
the door had been closed to you
a very long time ago!
Much later, I heard that, around that time,
you had passed away.

That dream haunted me
throughout the years.
Gradually,
the ice began melting.
A new sorrow
began emerging.
I finally realized that,
of all evil,
unforgiveness is the greatest one.
For if my loving Heavenly Father
could and does forgive me,
why not also forgive
my earthly father's failure
to show love to me?

30 March 2001

AN UNSURRENDERED HEART

It's a tug of war,
a fight for the dubious privilege
to sit on the throne of my heart.
Memories flashing past,
arousing,
caressing,
tempting.
Your face,
your hands,
even the way you walk
and the sweetness of the taste
of the forbidden fruit.
"Seek the things that are above".
Yet,
I revel in the soft autumn breeze,
the warm sunlight upon my face,
the rustling of the trees,
the white downy clouds
rushing across a cobalt sky,
the verdant fields and woods around me
and the memory of your love-
and the anticipated gamble
of its working out.

27 March 1984

AND I THOUGHT WE WERE FRIENDS!

After a night of too much food,
Champagne and "Krambambuli",
of seeming merriment
and quadruple fireworks displays,
I sit at my desk,
my heart tight
inside my chest.

We have spent a lifetime,
so it seems,
discussing our differing views.
For a long time,
they seemed to me
well humoured discussions,
though not lacking in conviction.

Lately though,
you have been throwing
fiery daggers of enmity
which I, unawares,
now incredulous
have allowed
to my very core.

Are you seeing me differently?
Or maybe only now
showing your true colours?
I have found it hard to believe
the seeming depth of your venom.
You always used to show courtesy-
contempt finally corroding that veneer.

Are we presently condemned
to relate in shallow merriment?
To dance around each other
in weary, cautious moves?
Or is this a long-overdue awakening
of a fact I tended to embellish?
That there never was substance from the start!

1 January 2005

AWAKENING

Again,
I had this wish
you might find me
and take me away,
to a life of awakening.

My feelings,
no longer asleep,
rather,
breaking forth
to escape this spell.

Your presence,
to me like the prince's kiss
for the timid Cinderella.
Springtime's scents and sights
finally restored to me.

The world,
now small and restricted,
opened up for us to be discovered.
You would even delay
the ebbing away of my youth.

In the end,
I waited in vain;
you are not seeking after me.
I heard you found someone else.
A new awakening put on hold once again.

Undated
(Probably late 1970's)

CARS PASSING

Drumming rain,
and the ebb and flow of cars passing.
Lying in the dark, waiting.

Your tears could not touch me.
Indifferent shame?
Why then these tears?
Nothing really matters.
It's all the same to me.
Tears and laughter.
Passion and indifference.
Day and night.
They all meet somewhere.
Now, I allow both to come.
Sometimes though, I forget.

The rain has ceased.
Only the sound of passing cars.
Lying in the dark, waiting.

November 1980

CAT AND MOUSE GAME

For so long,
I have sensed your pull
but put it down to mere attraction.

I have become tired
of playing games;
mere superficial outputs of the heart.

Yet,
that certain undefinable something
has remained.

Responding to you with coolness,
at times indifference;
finding myself on the receiving end of the same.

You have noticed me
foolishly giving my heart away,
only to receive it back bruised.

I can see,
we have been watching one another;
who's the cat and who's the mouse here?

My stance: detachment and slight irony.
Yours: uncanny and unnerving certainty,
or so it seems to me!

My view on this has changed now;
irony muted into uneasiness,
tinged with fear.

Worse still,
to my bewilderment and surprise-
I now am longing for your love and care!

My fear is that, as soon as you find out,
this victory might be all you were waiting for,
in order to turn your back on me!

9 August 1985

COCKROACHES

The room is like a cell.
Naked, white walls.
A bare bulb dangling,
shedding a cold, glaring light.
Black, shiny insects crawling around me.
Hundreds of cockroaches
swarming near me,
barely finding space.
Climbing over each other,
Then over my feet.

They fly against the walls,
dropping heavily to the ground.
A buzzing sea,
trying to engulf me.
Never ending chaos,
resonating within me.
Should I counter this creeping
with an act of desperate fury?
Not stopping,
till all have been crushed?

Now,
a door opens;
a call to quickly leave!
I brush off a few of the insects,
vigorously shake my head
and move my fingers through my hair.
Then run for the exit.
One last glance,
The door slams shut behind me.
I awake with a start.

Undated
(Probably around mid-1970's)

EMPTY

Sitting in the car,
waiting.
Empty.
All day talking-
untouched.
Laughter shared,
yet alone.
Game playing,
draining.
Discomfort,
best pushed away.
Complex pieces,
not fitting.
Longing
for harmony,
depth,
patterns matching,
colours blending,
truly relating,
connecting.
In vain.

28 July 1987

FAILED HARVEST

So much promise in that fruit!
Within it-
all the intensity
of a potential rich harvest.
Eagerly awaiting
the early rains,
the sun's warmth
and the earth's sustenance.

The rains were not due yet.
The sun's rays but weak
and the earth-
in its wintery sleep.
Bravely,
it persevered
with so much hope
and faith.

How long?
At some unknown point,
the point of no return,
that eager life within
started to let go.
Flickering, and gradually fading,
till it went out-
dropping to the ground.

That fruit was my undeclared love for you.
A love that nearly drove me to despair.
We were young then, too young.
Just when I could see a glimmer of hope-
life tore us apart.
Aging now and alone,
I mourn for that lost hope
of an early autumn harvest.

29 October 2012

FEELING RAW

Feeling raw,
as if coarse sandpaper
had been chafing my insides,
tearing up old wounds.

Expressing my pain
further worsens it
by your indignant denial,
adding disappointment to the mix.

Am I expected
to accept tokenistic caring?
Overt patronizing
and public humiliations?

I must rightly read what's there,
and see why I chose as I did.
Also, realize that no one deserves
to be treated such – no one!

Once fully accepted-
to take appropriate action,
whatever this action might be.
All I know: I deserve better!

I deserve better, **now**.
Not tomorrow, nor in the by and by.
Knowing this, will bring its own answer.
I don't fear what it may be.

10 October 2002

FOOL'S GOLD?

Some say,
"See how ugly he can be?
How much meanness,
even baseness is in him?
A coward,
and you know it!".
"Yes", she says.
"All this seems to be part of him,
I am aware of it.
Yet,
lately,
I have looked into a small window
of his heart,
usually kept tightly barricaded.
There,
I found kindness,
even a touch of beauty.
That's where I will put my hope.
I have witnessed his longing
for that hidden man within.
Only love can lead him to himself."
Like digging for gold-
some spend their all on fool's gold.
Some will persevere and find the real thing.

19 October 1978

FRAGMENTS

With a furious sword,
life has dashed to pieces
the core of his being.
Fragments are all that's left of him.

In a vain attempt at wholeness,
he seeks to find it in the fragment,
never knowing who he is.
Cynicism masking his brokenness.

His spirit asleep,
he is driven
by shifting sands,
rigidly adhering to external stability.

Could he but for a moment
look away from himself
and his unceasing quest,
a surprising thing may happen.

He could then see
that the very brokenness,
which fills him with hidden shame,
if embraced and surrendered, could bring life.

Weakness would be exchanged
for strength.
Ashes of grief and loss,
for the joy of new beginnings.

Simply, by laying down,
once and for all,
the old torn self
at the foot of the cross.

12 January 1993

FRIENDS

True and tried friends:
like shady trees,
on a hot summer's day.
Colourful flowers,
amongst rock and gravel.
A sweet drink with lots of ice,
after a long and weary walk.
Shiny ribbons and wrappings
around presents
under the Christmas tree.
Like waking up to a clear and sweet melody,
on a cool morning, in early Spring.
Or a dive in the pool,
after a hot and sticky day.
Even like a richly laid out banqueting table
you spot when first arriving at a dinner party.
In short, friends are the sugar and the spice
that make your life tasty, sweet and nice!

6 January 1987

FUTURE RESPONSE

No matter how endearing I may try to be-
I cannot control your future response!
For all I know and there is to see:
you're presenting your best side to me.

Once yours, will you turn from your kindness?
Anxious questions arise.
Drop your guard and reveal my blindness?
Disappointment to rob me of soundness?

Those smiling blue eyes in which I bask,
can they reveal if your love is real?
Can your poetry or your kisses, I ask?
And can you guarantee it will last?

I can decide to be true,
as I cannot guarantee your future response.
To continue to love and not be blue,
should loving response diminish from you.

31 November 1994

I KNOW

(Describing a relationship
I was watching close up)

Every time you leave me,
I die.

Though my death is not peace,
more like hell.
It is hopeless hope.

Then you come back–
and everything seems unreal:
my hell a mere illusion.
I don't understand it anymore.

Your presence–
a heavenly torture!
I know I have lost you.
I know what you feel
when you look at me that way.

I cling to you,
when you try to free yourself.
I try to charm you,
fully knowing
and reading in your eyes
that I have lost all charms.

I know how foolish,
to try to please you
when you are pushing me away.
I laugh, though I feel like crying.
It would only shorten your presence.
When you are gone, I will be free.
Then, my death will be complete.

London
February 1968

IMPROMPTU PERFORMANCE

On the sidewalk sits a lonely figure,
creating strange sounds
with his age old instrument.
Rapt in a trance,
strumming his chords,
while indifferent people rush past.
A group of adolescents
amuse themselves on nearby steps,
throwing coins into the musician's basket.
Grubby children stand around watching,
curiosity in their eyes.
The musician continues to play,
nodding when a coin is thrown.
His eyes gaze into nowhere.
A group of people stop and watch.
One of them slowly pulls out a flute
and continues to listen.
Then he brings it to his lips
and tentatively joins in.
Slowly unfolding between them,
a melody is created.
It steadily gains in liveliness,
until both instruments
merge into perfect harmony.
People stand still,
look puzzled,
then smile,
rocking to the music.

Byron Bay, New South Wales,
undated (80's)

JUST A DREAM

Last night,
I dreamt of you.
This morning,
again,
this strange consuming fire.
Do not worry my heart,
there is no fuel
to keep the fire burning.
You remain
unattainable as ever.
Soon,
those flames-
mere embers
and finally,
cold ash.
Once again,
the grey returns,
with its dull comfort.

Written in 1981

JUST FOR YOU

Have you ever felt
a feather-light breeze,
gently stirring your face?
Does a falling leaf,
at times,
lightly graze your cheek,
before it settles on the ground?
When you stretch out,
to absorb the last rays of a setting sun,
do you feel gentle warmth upon your skin?
And when snow falls,
do the dancing snowflakes
softly caress your face and hair?
It is my hand that's stretching out to you
and my fingers that softly stroke your skin.

Written in 1979

LIVING WITH UNEASINESS

What is this feeling in my pit?
This wrenching in my gut?
Like a knife turning.
Playing the blame game.
I catch that ball.
It weighs a ton!
Why catch it in the first place?

Like trying to lift a load,
too smooth to tackle.
Or turning a heavy mattress,
with no handles to hold.
Mountains,
or mole hills?
Merely an overactive mind?

Lying awake,
one more night.
In vain,
waiting for sleep to return.
I finally grab that little white pill.
It does for me
what I can't do for myself.

11 December 2007

LONGING

Alone in a hotel room,
he craves for her,
convinced that the immensity of his hunger
could not ever be satisfied.

Lying near her now,
he envisages a walk,
alone,
on a deserted beach.

Weary from yet another childbirth,
her hair in her eyes,
she gazes out into cold and stark whiteness,
her sick child finally asleep.

Hunched on a park bench,
the old spinster looks at the little child,
absorbed in a coloured leaf,
and forgets to throw bread to the pigeons.

Secretly,
the girl looks at the kissing lovers,
entwined in a primal embrace
and cannot fall asleep at night.

Her hands over her bulging body,
the young woman, longingly,
looks at the laughing schoolgirls,
passing near her window.

September 1978

LOST DREAMS

They robbed her of her dream
and smashed it in a hundred pieces.
For comfort, they made her believe
that it was a fake
of the real thing.

She used to find refuge in that dream.
Now she doesn't know
where to start looking for it.
Unexpectedly,
she finds one of the shattered pieces.

The rest have been dispersed
by a mocking wind,
irreparably so.
They have lost their dreams,
why shouldn't she?

Undated
Probably late 70's or early 80's

MAKING A STAND

Blank.
Flat.
Sitting alone
in a café,
after a futile confrontation.
We both agreed,
(not agreeably)
to disagree.

Two incidents,
involving
two (or too) differing people.
Two scenarios,
two attempts
at trying to shake
that
which cannot be shaken.

Should I feel bad
that some things
cannot be moved?
Why can't you accept
that sometimes,
I need to make a stand?
A stand is a stand.
Not a shuffle.

Could it be that those
who don't want to make a stand,
resent mostly those
who can and do?
Today, I slammed the door
on half-hearted apologies,
on past & present berating
and on a litany of expectations.

30 March 2001

NO ONE TOLD ME BACK THEN

No one told me
what I should have been told
about love.
Natural attraction
should not be the determining factor
to make a final choice.
Life-long commitment
requires loyalty, selflessness
and endurance, in order to last.
I needed to be careful,
in order not to sell myself short
and not miss the very best.

To guard my heart,
the most precious thing
about myself.
The state of my heart
dictating the quality of my life.
Instead, these memories-
a mixture of bitter sweet.
More bitter, than sweet.
I could have been spared
much heartache and tears.
But then again...
no one really understood back then!

5 October 2012

ODE TO A SOUL-MATE DREAM

While away,
with much time on my hands
to think and write,
I find myself re-reading
ancient love letters of mine to you,
given back to me;
an encounter with a young self.

Between the lines,
a persistent theme,
a thread,
repeatedly leading me astray.
A dream,
which has followed me
all my life.

A sweet foretaste
of that which didn't come to pass;
to find and deeply love
that much anticipated soul-mate.
Instead,
I hold these letters of dreams,
returned to me- they didn't seem to fit.

My mother,
who hardly knew me,
nor made the time,
called me
"nothing but a dreamer".
Dreams
without substance?

If she knew,
she didn't show me
how to manage dreams.
Unknowingly,
could she have been
pouring contempt
on her own broken dreams?

As for me,
those dreams were mine alone,
my own responsibility.
Foolishly,
I tried to make them yours as well.
Lacking the insight
that they needed to fit us both!

Did I believe then
that love alone
would surely put it right?
Remove all obstacles?
Was I saturated
by dangerous lies,
presented to us on the movie screen?

What I found instead
was that love
is needed mainly
to bring release.
Professions of undying love,
couldn't even stop the insult
of the wandering eye.

Strange,
how two separate honeymoons
like omens,
were spent with husbands,
both on sickbeds.
Walking in honeymoon gardens,
alone.

Today,
I heard the call
to put that broken dream
finally to rest.
It felt like a part of me
being ripped out
of my heart.

The hope
of finding fulfilment
of that long-held desire,
and the anticipation of ensuing sweetness-
for both of us.
Almost unbearable,
to part with that life-long dream!

Even now, that I am aging,
it will not willingly go.
Except for that call
to a new and higher dream,
which must stand alone.
Demanding
all others to be put to death.

This dream-
A King's dream
for His beloved Bride.
His call-
Arise, to taste of His love
and to let Him lead,
despite the dying involved.

I will wait for Him,
and seek Him
with new hope in my heart.
"Winter is past",
He says,
"the rains are over and gone".
Spring is here.
(Song of Songs 2:11-13).

Culburra Beach, New South Wales
12 October 2012

PAIN

All through the night,
I listen to the struggled breathing
of my feverish child.
When I call your name,
there is no answer.
I go near your bed-
greyness
the expression of your face.
Empty and withering,
I want to release
these choking feelings,
without being able
to shed one single tear.
Most painful of all:
feeling
and being made to feel
that the cause of all this,
lies inside
my very own self!

Undated, 1978 approx.

PLAYING WITH FIRE

The dreams she can read in his eyes
no longer are about her.
The silence between them
doesn't speak of togetherness.
The love songs they listen to
won't draw them together.
Even the full moon he contemplates
takes him far from her.
Everything that brought him close to her,
now pushes him away further.

I can see all this;
that I am pulling him away from her.
Playing with fire-
of a dangerous kind.
I know full well, right from wrong.
This belongs to the latter.
Yet I cannot
will not,
cease searching for his eyes
and bathe in the warmth they radiate.

(Undated, probably 1984 or earlier)

PREDATOR

We talked about love.
A surprise visitor;
a friend of friends
and I, his host,
giving him a lift
to the station.
I talked about Agape-
the most powerful force
in all the universe!
He just laughed.
I could detect
embarrassment
in his laughter.

My friends failed to disclose:
Passion,
this he knew.
Obsession,
his daily bread.
Perversion,
a preferred trademark.
In typical predatory style,
well known to his kind,
I later realized-
he had tried to proposition
my beautiful twelve-year old
to go with him to a distant land!

30 March 1988

QUITTING

You think you've got reasons
to quit.
"Always a looser",
you state.
"Tried,
for a long time now-
No go!"
That makes two of us.
"Some never get a fair go",
you say.
"Crippled",
you call it,
"before we could walk".
What's new?
You put the blame
on your world.
"Dog eats doggy",
and so on.
You feel like
crawling into a hole
and falling asleep,
for a very long time.
So do I.
Then again-
the only losers
are quitters!

31 July 1987

RED CARNATIONS

(Dedicated to Betty Carver)

Your garden's red carnations
exude a perfume from long ago.
They evoke childhood memories,
when flowers were uniquely different;
not just by looks but also by scent.

Old fashioned red carnations-
simple, unobtrusive.
Not like the showy roses,
nor the exotic profusion of orchids.
They are happy to bloom in everyday gardens.

These red carnations,
unlike jasmine and wisteria,
whose perfume is heady and pervasive;
their scent is appreciated only
by those who would draw near.

Your gift of red carnations,
a token to gladden my heart and soul,
have a sweetness that is constant.
They are a perfect expression
of your friendship and love.

16 December 2002

SECRET GARDEN

Come with me
to a grand tour
of my secret garden.

I give you the key
to the old iron gate,
inside the wall.

The perfume of honeysuckle,
overhanging the wall,
permeates the air.

You may bring
a jar of your tears
and whispers of your heart.

Leave such weights as fear-
shadows of the night,
at the foot of the gate.

As you wander through the garden,
I will be there beside you
discovering anew its secrets.

Water abounds in my garden.
It lies sleepily in quiet ponds
and sings merrily in winding brooks.

At times, they turn into raging torrents,
which could sweep you away,
together with leaves and branches.

Deep within the center of the garden,
dark and jagged crevices loom.
Remnants of past tremors and devastation.

I'll lead you safely around those.
Just hold my hand;
we will need to tread softly there.

My garden isn't all sweet and serene.
Intruders will find it treacherous,
whereas you are my welcome guest.

December 1994

SIMPLY THANK YOU

Dear one,
I want to thank you,
while the clouds,
like the curtain on a stage,
have been pulled back,
allowing the sun-rays to break through.
Thank you for taking me
to see the thundering sea,
the towering peaks
and the glens of ferns,
gently quivering in the misty rain.
Thank you for showing me
the rare and solitary orchid,
hidden amongst rocks
and thorny shrubs.
For the laughter,
the cups of coffee,
sitting on windy hillsides,
overlooking a sea of trees,
or crashing waves.
For your letters,
tenderly describing
the sky,
Fish River,
and creatures,
appearing unexpectedly.
For those poet's words of yours,
causing my rusty heart strings
to reverberate to the tune
of a symphony in the making.

Thank you for holding on,
through those howling storms,
which put Tracey to shame.
For your cupped hands
around the wildly flickering flame.
Thank you.

                                                  28.12.1995

SUBSTITUTES

Grasping
for glitter.
A brief struggle to get;
when finally won,
the interest is gone.

Not daring
to believe
for that which really satisfies.
Instead, elbowing
for short-lived substitutes.

Undated
Possibly written in 1980's

TENTS DANCING

Hot, dry wind
over parched desert land,
swirling up sand,
stinging eyes and partly exposed faces-
mainly of women and children,
queuing for their daily rations.
A sea of tents,
as far as the eye can see.
Makeshift homes for refugees;
once large families
with a desire to prosper,
to give a future to their offspring.
Also, to offer shelter
to their aging parents,
and to enjoy status
in their communities.
War tore them asunder;
killing, raping and maiming,
indiscriminately.
Presently,
reduced to the status of beggars.
A perceived burden.
A political football.
Stateless
and homeless.
Their dignity left behind.
After the numbness of grief,
what is there left
but blame?
Easy targets
for ideologies of hatred.

Usually,
towards "meddlers from the West"!
They came with guns and tanks
and a self-righteous demeanour.
They are usually the ones
now offering charity,
expecting gratitude.
Why not bite the hand,
perceived to have held a gun?
When hatred prevails,
truth becomes irrelevant.
Whose truth, anyway?
The war may have been left behind
but is now raging
in wounded human hearts.
As quick as it arose
the wind has died down.
The shimmering heat
causing tents to dance,
on waves of scorching sand.

29 September 2013

THE ALLY

After yet another night of tossing,
the revelation
that I have lost my ally,
since losing your favour.

I have concluded
that it is too costly
trying to humour you
on a continuous basis.

"What kind of ally?"
I asked myself.
"Why should I need an ally?"
Questions not asked before.

Have I been living
with a warped raison d'être?
Some phobic angst maybe,
about "them and us"?

My unannounced appearance-
an unwanted 'baby bump',
forced my parents to take a step
which eventually undid us all.

Every which way,
both turned away from me.
Gone were what should have been
my greatest allies.

Other carers too busy
with their own lives.
Fickle allies, to be sure.
Allies and accusers, all in one.

The more allies then,
the more chance
to keep the pointing at bay?
You seem to practice this belief.

By not humouring your outlook,
I end up in opposition.
Expressions of our hidden fears
towards one another.

This warped perception
and warlike inner stance
only thrives in the darkness
of our hidden primeval fears.

Presently, as for me,
I have two allies only
against ignorance
and inner and outer lies.

God, who died for me
and I,
who made a pact with self:
always "to thine own self be true"!

Undated, possibly December 1998

THE APPENDIX

The lie
of their perception
and of the gradual becoming
a mere appendix.
An extension of someone else.

Trying to connect,
only to realize;
all I shall ever be
in their eyes-
just an appendix.

A part of the real thing,
of the desired one,
of the one that matters.
The inner circle will only connect
with their own kind.

I see it
and then I don't.
The inner ache reminds me;
there cannot be connection
when you're on the outer.

To simply love is not enough;
mere tolerance- all you get in return.
To want to be loved by all
is naïve in the extreme,
a recipe for pain.

Looking in all the wrong places,
that foolish little child
is led astray by a smile.
Driven by blind hunger
to belong and to be loved.

Why then stay where hunger
only gets crumbs?
Why dwell at the edge of starvation
where the disguised face of lack
exalts the meagre fare?

Instead of searching
for that which sustains,
it seems easier
to just…
keep barely alive.

A clever ploy or diabolical scheme
in order to keep one in fetters
while feeding them lies?
Weaving gossamer blankets
that cannot give warmth.

Trying to convince
that the hunger
is really satiation.
The cold merely the result
of a distorted reality.

18 October 2003

THE BIRTH

Part of our training-
witnessing my first birth!
Painfully aware of cold white walls,
glaring lights over a writhing woman's body,
held and surrounded by those in charge.

An oppressive picture
of crushing humiliation;
bloodstained sheets
and agonized screams-
I turn my head away.

A wave of excitement now.
The peak of expectation can be felt.
Raised voices from the staff,
giving instructions to the mother.
Rapidly increasing, a dark mass emerging.

A small head,
growing into shoulders,
chest and arms,
and soon into a slimy,
slippery human being.

"The matching outcome
of this labour of ugliness",
my ignorant self concludes.
Soon the room is filled
with a loud and miserable sound.

I shiver at the coldness around me.
All I want is for this to be over.
Then I look at the mother
stretching out her hands,
holding the noisy bundle against her.

I cannot take my eyes off her face.
All agony vanished from it.
Instead,
there is a light,
a smile so gentle.

Her hands stroking the baby,
seem strong and warm.
Again, I turn away my head;
to hide the tears
that secretly roll down my face.

July 1979

THE DIARY

Dedicated to Roland

Seeing life's autumn creep up on me,
the need arose
to finally bring closure
to an old flame of mine.

The impetus–
an old re-surfaced diary
which opened up a Pandora's Box,
filled with longing and pain.

Anew, knocked off my feet!
Why this intensity?
Who was this boy,
evoking such uncaused pain?

Why could I never speak to him?
A search commenced
to finally get some answers.
And lo! A response!

Back then, I should have known
and now discovered:
Like Dante and Beatrice,
my existence- unknown to him!

Worse than Tillandsia,
I had fed on airy hopes
and future projection:
distorted images of love.

Then, the sum-total
of life's primary relationships.
Throughout early life-
abuse, neglect and abandonment.

Lately, bullying and ridicule-
my daily diet.
Fear of rejection-
my safe hiding place.

People had been cruel;
my image of him- Christ-like.
A bubble that wouldn't burst,
if not touched.

Fifty years later,
the bubble finally burst;
a strange, liberating emptiness lingering.
An after-taste of death.

Death, made up of past toxic pain,
wrong beliefs
and distorted, illusionary thinking
about love.

Later, experiences of pseudo-love
and destructive love games.
The fake is recognized only
by knowing the real first.

Now, all safely nailed to the cross.
Not mysterious religion
but life-giving reality,
being in Christ, through faith.

Not returning to fantasy and make-believe
but touched by the Real.
Continuously receiving life-changing,
life-enhancing and life-supporting grace.

I put the lock back on my diary,
the lid on the empty Pandora's Box
and added one more chapter
to the story of my life.

6 March 2013

THE GUARDIAN

Today
I said adieu
to my old guardian.
A legacy of my childhood
I had been clinging to
for far too long.
He served me well,
keeping those bullies at bay,
teasing and taunting me,
waiting for me in alleyways
during my school years.
The timid victim,
after reading
a certain book,
turned into a war machine,
driven by indignant rage,
showing them what they were:
mere cowards at best!

I now realize
this build-up of anger,
once unleashed
causes untold damage
to self and others.
There are better ways
to deal with
seeming wrongs.
Anger felt
needs to be acknowledged.
Anger expressed,
carefully filtered.

The instinctive response
replaced
with a God-inspired
and adult one.
Time to grow up
a little bit more.

The Old Covenant of law
has been fulfilled
by the new covenant of grace.
The time has come
to bravely let go of the old
and entrust myself
to the Safe Keeper
of faith and trust.
Injuries
keep turning up.
Insults
make their way to my door.
It happens to all.
How to continue to respond?
My default mode
isn't the way of life in Him now.
His life
must and will come forth!

28 January 2008

My Best Poems — Part 2 – RELATIONSHIPS

THE IDOL

"Trust me," he said.
I tried, in vain.
He didn't measure up.
Didn't conform.
Didn't fit the mould.
The pattern of the image which,
long ago,
I put my trust in.
When realized,
it would fulfil all my hopes.
Releasing the woman within.
The hoped for cast of man,
w
h
i
c
h

n
o
w

h
a
d

b
e
c
o
m
e
mere idolatry.

5 August 1996

THE MASQUERADE

I went to a masquerade,
where everyone followed the rules-
except me.

All busy acting their part,
happy and with abandon-
except me.

"How ridiculous their disguise", I thought.
"They are only fooling themselves-
except me."

"I will resist and show conviction.
Some might take off the mask they're wearing-
except me."

Then one of them, with amused expression,
with a sweeping gesture
bowed very low in front of me.

"Your courage is admirable".
"No doubt, I would follow your example,
but for one thing:

You lack gaiety, nor feel at ease.
You might convince someone else-
except me!"

20 February 1976

THE ROAD TO FREEDOM

Unkindness and evil abound,
leaving torment and misery
in their wake,
making life a burden.
The soft heart of a child changed
into the stony heart of mankind.

The word you used was "scum".
"None worth a crumpet,
treacherous at every turn,
the more of them you get to know!"
An expert at protective self-deception,
you simply don't trust anyone!

Attracted to the ones in kind,
you feel to be the wise one,
having figured it all out,
boasting of outsmarting "them".
Laughing at those foolish ones, talking of love.
"Airheads!" Yet their serenity unnerves you.

Hard, cunning, yet straining at the reel.
Feeling disliked and deeply lonely.
"Ah, what rubbish!" you say.
"Just a touch of lingering sentimentality,
probably instilled by mushy aunts at babyhood."
And, "We are men and men are made of steel!"

Your sons, while little, had many fears.
They were too soft, you said.
They needed toughening up.
You mocked them for their frailty.
Softness would not survive in this harsh world.
They hid in shame and cried bitter tears.

Not only did they hide from softness –
they also hid from you!
You counted on them becoming like you
but got a simmering hatred instead.
They had become hard alright!
Directed at you was their loathing.

Loneliness grasped you with its iron clasp.
Self-doubt found your Achilles heel.
Sudden bursts of rage,
in-between dark brooding.
Lingering over drink,
your bitterness an ever deepening cesspool.

Finally, you had to admit:
"Where did I go wrong?"
The pain you felt was the pain of death,
which has a way of breaking us,
if we cannot bend with it.
Wisdom waiting to bring life out of ashes.

"Still Waters", Budgewoi
8 February 2005

THE TOXIC PARENT

How can seeming kindness
be so toxic?
Is it that it has more to do
with the giver,
than with the one given to?
The charity syndrome,
which enhances the giver,
at the expense of the receiver?
An unspoken "you should be grateful!"
ringing in my ears.
With all that giving,
I become the poorer,
more disempowered.
Feeling less capable
and more inadequate.
Maybe, it is to do
with your unceasing attempt
to teach me
your so-called better ways.
The trouble is-
I feel so undervalued.
Handicapped
in your eyes.
One such remark
triggers a thousand memories.

I gaze into mirrors,
of mirrors,
of mirrors,
down the hallway of time.
To you,
I still seem
the untimely fruit
of your body.
The embarrassment
of your past.
The blemish
that won't go away.
Is that why
you cannot let me be me?

Zurich, Switzerland
15 October 2005

TIME

Already,
time is eroding
the memory
of you.

Your presence,
once an inseparable part of me,
now moving away
from me.

The once piercing pain
tearing at my heart,
becoming dull
with the passing of time.

Your image,
just recently
sharp and strong,
becoming blurred.

Straining
to remember
the traits
of your face.

Where there was trust,
more and more doubts arising.
"We need to grow, separately,
each one in our own way."

This is what you said.
I only hope
we won't grow
apart.

Undated
Probably late 1970's

TO WRITE POETRY

Surrounded by dusty furniture,
fresh washing to be folded,
dry and droopy flowers in a vase,
and dirty dishes in the sink–
the urge to write poetry!

Despite insistent cries from hungry cats,
circling and rubbing around my legs,
the guilt of unanswered letters,
and bills spilling out everywhere-
the irresistible pull to write poetry!

Despite uncertainty,
as to worth and skill
of my unpolished art,
playful and untamable-
the choice to write poetry!

5 March 1995

TOUCHED BY THE DIVINE

(A Prophetic Poem)

A shy young woman's unrequited love.
Sighing and tears unending,
falling on barren ground.
Later, tossed and twisted
by life's chaotic events.

A whirlwind of demands,
gradually
spiraling downward.
Greying hair,
slowing step.

Finally,
pen in hand,
processing those events.
The memory of that distant love,
re-awakening pain and grief.

Daring now
and curious.
Did he ever know?
Locating him –
easier than she thought.

A surprised but open response.
From a distance
she finally finds out
that he never knew her,
nor of her love back then.

In a poem to him
she shares
about her love now,
for the One
Who loves them both.

The One
whose picture
was marred for him
by religion back then,
when she loved him.

Her plea to him now:
'Dare to look beyond
that false portrait'.
This encounter
deeply touches him.

Gradually,
his initial reluctance ebbing away.
In its stead,
discovering a hidden treasure,
filling a void that had always been there.

By an act of divine grace,
those seemingly wasted tears,
anointed by the Divine
become rivers of life that now bring eternity
to a soul otherwise forever lost.

6 July 2014

(Vision given by revelation,
believed in faith)

"Nearly all of God's jewels are crystallized tears." Anon

TRANSITION

She is looking for freedom
but to the first lover
she gives away her heart.
She wants to expand,
to reach out.
Then, at the first cold wind,
she runs for shelter.
She says she never feels lonely,
why then is she waiting so anxiously
for his step to approach?
She says it doesn't matter if he won't come.
That she will laugh at her own crazy dreams.
Why then does her laughter cease
when the music stops?

Undated, approx. 1980's

TRUE VINE COMMUNITY

A Chapter in my Life

Middle Pocket was a hamlet.
"Beulah" a tiny farmhouse,
in the middle of paddocks,
strewn with ample cow dung,
drying in the scorching sun.
A creek running through it,
thorny blackberries bordering it.
A mouse once popped out of a drain,
in the middle of my shower!
All around neighbours,
living the alternate lifestyle.
Growing veggies,
harvesting fresh chicken eggs,
spinning and weaving,
and looking the part!
Walking home after a visit,
on a deserted country road,
pitch black and moonless,
except for the generous spread
of a crystal clear Milky Way
and its cohort.
Drenching rain, at times
caused creeks to overflow,
submerging bridges.
Surrounded by water-
house-bound!

Children celebrating,
"No school today!
Neither tomorrow,
till the waters subside".
Dave, a tall lanky Canadian,
with the most likeable laughter;
I was smitten straightaway.
Les the pastor,
a mixture of Jesus
and a gentle Indian guru,
attentive in conversation.
Plenty of young single mums
and their children,
sharing houses.
We felt safe and nurtured.
Many young married couples.
A few single men.
Sadly, no grey crowns,
to add needed life experience.
Most, from a hippy background;
once growing and smoking dope,
vegging out in Nimbin
and surrounds.
Our own school,
part of the church setup.
Many, encouraged to volunteer
one day a week.
Visiting the hills of Mullum,
a sudden revelation
of a process occurring in me,
which I defined later
as "group-think";
a "them and us" mind-set.

Alarm bells going off
in my mind.
The lingering stench
of cultism,
later quickly forgotten,
only to return with a vengeance,
when a bomb was dropped.
Suddenly, all leaders disbanded,
replaced by those from the city.
A new and unknown bunch.
Sheep scattered to the four winds.
Some returned to their old ways.
I moved house, withdrew
and wrote poetry.
There I met a couple;
leaders in hiding,
wounded by dysfunction
in their church.
A different church.
And I quickly grew up.

11 October 2013

WAITING

Where is that someone,
not just anyone?
Free,
untangled,
mature,
ready
to make our relationship
a priority.

Recognizing
and fully aware
that such a relationship
and commitment
is what he wants,
even longs for.
Awake to the price
and willing to pay it.

While waiting,
I will fill my mind
and heart
with Him,
the Giver of all good things,
who gives bread to the hungry
and water to the thirsty.
Time is in His hands.

January 1993

WITHOUT A VOICE

A child abandoned.
Carers, too busy to hear
the crying in the night.
Without comfort,
eventually,
the crying ceased-
a hopeless giving up.
Left without a voice.

The little child, perceived to be
not too little to be left alone.
Detected by a roaming predator.
Beguiled by interest shown,
then entrapped by a web of threats.
The horror and defilement
by filth personified.
Left without a voice.

The fragile balance lost.
Threats echoing.
Fear in the field
and fear at night.
Tortured dreams.
Drawing pictures perverse.
Can anybody hear her silent screams?
Left without a voice.

Adults too busy
to cope with her obvious needs.
No one to show her
how to resolve those painful things.
All she gets is blame
and its resultant shame.
Unawares, she swallows that bitter pill.
Left without a voice.

Tossed like a rag-doll
from home to home.
Tolerating her,
as long as it suits them.
No one to take responsibility,
nor to make the commitment
to offer the warmth of a stable home.
Left without a voice.

The last attempt at care
consists of a regime of ridicule,
whenever she voices her thoughts.
Whether it be some issue at school
or bullies waiting on her way home,
the reply usually consists of blame,
reinforcing her sense of abandonment.
Left without a voice.

Time has passed.
She is now fifty-eight.
Why is she feeling so low tonight?
There have been triggers.
Voices from the past.
Is that how she used to feel?
Does this feeling have a name?
Yes, left without a voice!

Zurich, Switzerland
5 November 2005

YOU AND I

Two cliffs,
separated by a chasm-
you and I.
The chasm, fear.
You,
driven by the old fear
of not being loved.
Demanding
tokens of love.

As if that would satiate!
My fear:
being deprived of the freedom
to love freely.
Instead,
the heavy weight of expectations,
robbing joy in giving.
The risk is too great for you;
by letting go of control
you might end up
with nothing at all!
You cling to the illusion
that this will ensure
the quenching of thirst.
Sadly,
all you will ever get
is an unsteady trickle.
To get a gushing stream:
fear replaced
with appreciation-
trusting and embracing
my right to learn
to love you freely.

Easter 2002